You Are in Ancient Rome

Ivan Minnis

Raintree

Chicago, Illinois

Customer Service 888-363-4266

Visit our website at www.raintreelibrary.com

Illustrated by Jeff Edwards
Printed and bound in China by the South China
Printing Company

09 08 07 06 05
10 9 8 7 6 5 4 3 2 1

**Library of Congress
Cataloging-in-Publication Data:**
Minnis, Ivan.
  You are in ancient Rome / Ivan Minnis.
     p. cm. -- (You are there!)
  Audience: Ages 7-9.
  Includes index.
  Contents: The Roman empire -- Meet the
Romans -- The city streets -- Roman farms -- A
Roman feast -- Life for children -- Reading and
writing -- Roman art -- Technology --
Entertainment -- Roman rulers -- Roman religion.
  ISBN 1-4109-0618-3 (library binding-hardcover) -
- ISBN 1-4109-1010-5 (pbk.)
  1. Rome--Civilization--Juvenile literature. 2.
Rome--Social life and customs--Juvenile literature.
[1. Rome--Civilization. 2. Rome--Social life and
customs.] I. Title. II. Series: You are there
(Chicago, Ill.)
DG78.M64 2005
937--dc22
            2003027744

Acknowledgments
The author and publishers are grateful to the
following for permission to reproduce copyright
material: p. 4 Paul Bale; p. 5, 6 AKG Images,
photograph by Erich Lessing; p. 7B, 9L, 9R, 12, 19
John Seely; p. 7T, 13, 14, 15, 18R Ancient Art &
Architecture; p. 8, 16, 26T Trevor Clifford; p. 10
Corbis/Polypix, Eye Ubiquitous; p. 11 Ancient Art
& Architecture, photograph by R. Ashworth; p.
17, 23 Terry Griffiths & Magnet Harlequin; p. 18L,
25, 26B, 29 Ancient Art & Architecture,
photograph by R. Sheridan; p. 20, 22 Corbis; p. 24
AKG Images; p. 27 AKG Images, photograph by
Gilles Mermet; p. 28 Corbis, photograph by
Araldo de Luca

Cover photograph by James Davis Travel
Photography

The publisher would like to thank Elizabeth West
for her comments in the preparation of this book.

Every effort has been made to contact copyright
holders of any material reproduced in this book.
Any omissions will be rectified in subsequent
printings if notice is given to the publisher.

Contents

Any words appearing in bold, **like this,** are explained
in the glossary.

The Roman Empire

Two thousand years ago there were many great cities and **civilizations** around the world. In Central America the Zapotecs and Mayans ruled much of the land. In Asia, China was growing strong. Around the Mediterranean Sea, the civilizations of ancient Egypt and Greece had declined. They had become part of another huge **empire,** the Roman Empire.

Rome was a small farming community in Italy that became one the greatest empires of all time. As it grew rich it began to take over other lands.

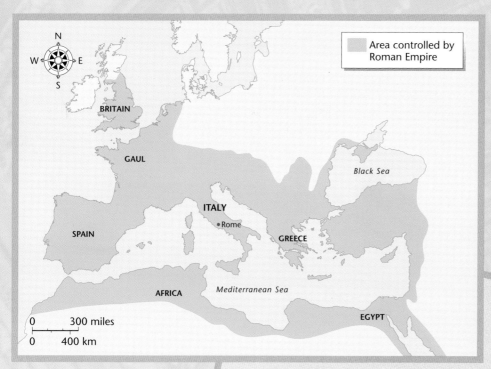

This map shows the Roman Empire at around 117 C.E., when Romans ruled over most of Europe and North Africa.

Two thousand years ago, the Roman Empire stretched from modern day Great Britain to North Africa, from modern day Spain to Israel.

Exploring the Empire

In this book you will travel back in time to ancient Rome. You will see what life was like in the time of Augustus, one of the greatest Roman **emperors**. You will visit the busy towns and meet their people. Get ready for the sights and sounds of the ancient world.

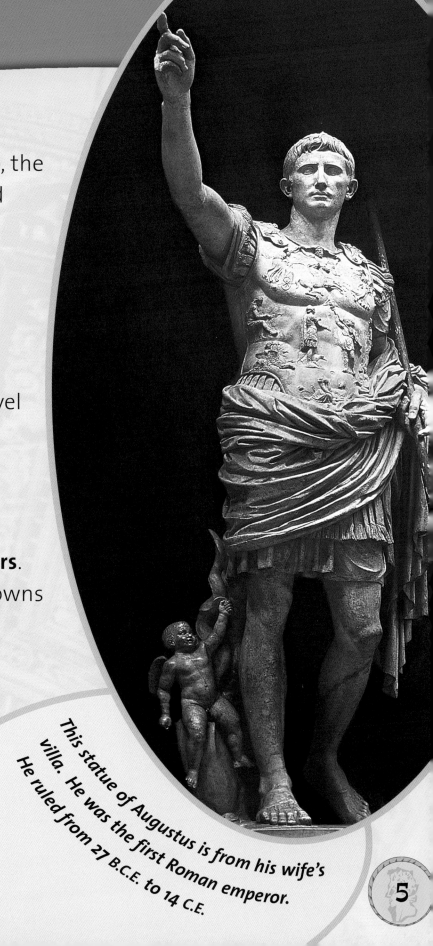

This statue of Augustus is from his wife's villa. He was the first Roman emperor. He ruled from 27 B.C.E. to 14 C.E.

Meet the Romans

Imagine making your way through the crowds on a busy Roman street. Rich businessmen wear long cloaks called togas. Rich married women wear a dress called a stola. Stolas have many different colors. The rich women also wear makeup, perfume, and fine jewelry.

The city streets are full of ordinary people who work hard for a living. Some work in small shops, serving the people of the great city. These people dress much more simply than the rich. The men wear short **tunics** with a cloak in cold weather. The women wear a stola made of plain brown or gray cloth. Children wear short tunics so that they can run and play.

Wealthy men wear togas. They are made from a single piece of cloth, which is draped around the body.

Slaves

There are also many slaves. They come from all across the **Empire** and are brought to Rome to work for the **citizens.** They can be bought and sold by their owners and many live a very hard life.

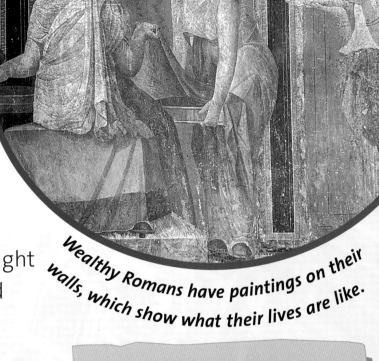

Wealthy Romans have paintings on their walls, which show what their lives are like.

Learning about Roman clothes

The Romans left many beautiful statues that show us how people dressed and their hairstyles. Wall paintings and **mosaics** show us the colors they used for clothing.

Wealthy Romans often had their portraits painted. This painting shows a lawyer and his wife from Pompeii.

The City Streets

Rome is the largest city in the world. The most important building is the **forum.** This is where people come to buy and sell their goods. People also hold meetings here. Shops and cafés line the streets leading away from the forum. Above them are apartments, where ordinary families live. Only the rich can live in the big houses on the hill next to the forum.

Horses and cattle pull heavy carts to bring goods in and out of the city. Some streets have stepping stones to keep your feet out of the garbage and animal waste that flows down the street.

Roman cities are built around the forum. The center of the Empire is the forum in Rome.

Stepping stones allow people to cross the muddy streets. Spaces are left for cart wheels to pass through.

Shops line the streets. Bread is baked and sold at bakeries like this.

Taking a bath

Everyone goes to bathhouses to relax, as well as for washing. You wash yourself in a series of big baths, like swimming pools. Some have hot water, others are freezing cold.

Learning about towns: Pompeii

In 79 C.E. a volcano called Mount Vesuvius erupted and covered the town of Pompeii in ash and dust. Nearly 1,700 years later, people uncovered the town. The ash preserved Pompeii so well that in some houses you can still see paintings on the walls.

9

Roman Farms

In the countryside farmers grow food for the people in the cities. You can see many different crops in different parts of the Empire. In Italy and North Africa the weather is hot and dry. Here olives are grown for their oil. Grapes are grown to make wine. In Northern Europe the weather is much cooler and wetter. Vegetables such as cabbages and carrots are grown there. Animals such as cattle and sheep are kept for meat. Cattle provide milk and sheep's wool is used to make clothing.

There are Roman villas, or farms, all over Europe. This one is in Britain.

People in the country also hunt for animals such as wild boar and deer.

Life at a villa

Many farms are owned by very rich **landowners.**
They live in huge villas while all of the hard work is
done by poor farmworkers and slaves. Plows pulled by
oxen are used to prepare the ground for planting crops.
At harvest time, the farmworkers have to spend the day
bent over to harvest the crop by hand. Sometimes the
whole family has to work in the hot and dusty fields.

A Roman Feast

Most Roman families eat very simple meals. Women run the household. They are experts at making sure that no food is wasted. You might have lentils and beans, which are made into a stew and eaten with bread. You will rarely eat meat because it is expensive. A fish sauce called garum is very popular. It is left out in the sun to make it smell very strong and fishy. You can add it to your food to give it more taste.

The Romans cook over charcoal, like a barbeque. This is a kitchen stove from Pompeii.

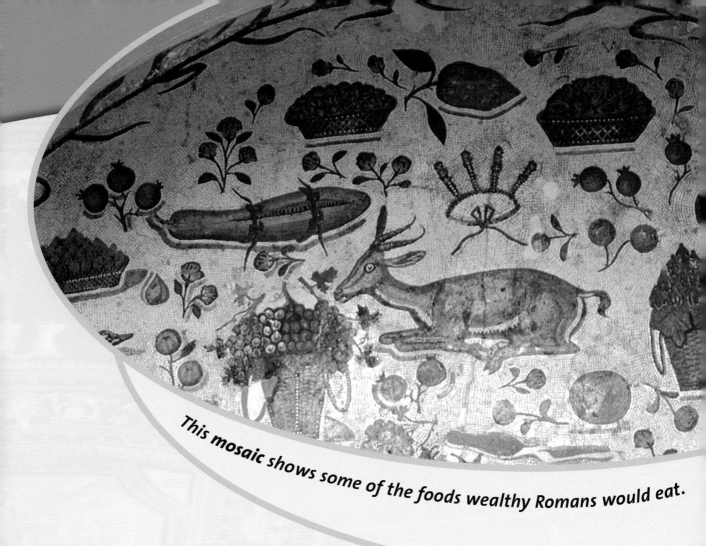

This mosaic shows some of the foods wealthy Romans would eat.

Fine food

The rich eat very different food than the poor. They only eat one main meal a day, but this is often a big feast. It starts around four in the afternoon, but can last for several hours. People eat sitting and lying on couches around a table. Slaves prepare several unusual courses. For example, songbirds may be served in an asparagus sauce, and you may be offered rodents cooked in honey. There is always plenty of fresh fruit, like figs and grapes.

Life for Children

If you are from a poor family you will not go to school. You also will not have a lot of time to play. Children start working when they are very young. Even a four year old is expected to do his or her share.

Life for a rich child is better, but still tough. Boys and some girls are sent to school. School begins early in the morning and finishes at noon. Children are expected to learn things by heart and can be punished for making mistakes. However they have more time for play than poor children. Girls do not go to school after the age of twelve. They stay at home to learn about running a home from their mothers.

These boys are playing a ball game. They are probably wealthy because poor children do not have much time to play.

Families

Roman fathers are in charge of their family completely. Girls are often expected to get married at about thirteen years old. They have to marry someone picked by their parents. A Roman father is very powerful when his children are adults, too.

Roman girls learn how to run the household from their mothers.

Reading and Writing

There are people from all over the **Empire** in Rome. You will hear them speaking a lot of different languages. The Romans have their own language, Latin. Latin is spoken by anyone who wants to be important in the Empire. The sons of wealthy Romans learn it at school, or are taught it at home by slaves who are trained as tutors.

Many languages are spoken in the Empire. Latin is spoken in Rome and used for official documents.

Learning Latin

The Latin language only has 22 letters and is always written in capitals. If you learn to write Latin, you will use a special pen called a stylus to scratch letters on to **wax tablets.** The tablets can be melted down and used again.

Only important people can write on paper using pens made from **reeds** and ink from soot. All around the city there are stones carved with letters. Some tell stories while others show the names of streets and buildings.

Only important people can write on paper using simple pens dipped in ink made from soot.

Learning about Latin

Latin has been used to make up many of the words we use today. Here are some Latin words, with the English word we use now:

Latin	English
circus	circle
non	not
musica	music

Roman Art

All over the **Empire** you will see that many public buildings are decorated with statues and carvings. Roman **emperors** like to have statues of themselves in the cities. They show the people how powerful they are. **Temples** have images of the gods who are worshipped there. The public bathhouses may have statues and **mosaics** of Neptune, god of the sea.

This mosaic shows a guard dog. Beware of the dog!

Ancient Rome has many statues honoring Roman gods and goddess

This painting is from the home of a wealthy Roman. It shows Bacchus, the god of wine.

Art at home

If you enter the house of a wealthy Roman family, you will see art all around you. These homes often have beautiful floors covered with **mosaics.** Mosaics are pictures made with thousands of tiny tiles. Different scenes are painted on the walls of the house. Sometimes you might see a picture of the people who own the house.

There are also craftspeople who make beautiful jewelry, pots, and metalwork. These are sometimes slaves. They have been brought from all over the Empire to produce works of art for the people of Rome.

Roman Machines

The Romans are famous for their engineers. **Aqueducts** carry clean water across valleys to the cities. Builders use simple tools like hammers, chisels, and saws but they are able to put up huge buildings. They are very careful about the measurements they use.

The homes of some rich people have running water and even central heating! Hot air is passed through spaces under floors and in gaps in walls. A slave has to work hard to keep the furnace hot to warm the air.

Huge aqueducts like this one in France carry water to the busy Roman cities.

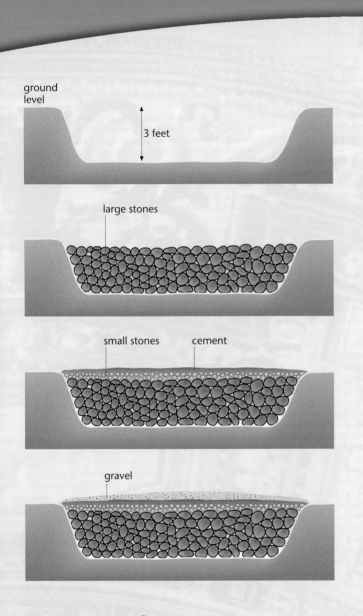

ground level

3 feet

large stones

small stones   cement

gravel

Smooth straight Roman roads make traveling much easier.

Learning about technology

Many Roman buildings were so well built that we can still see them today, 2,000 years later. They can teach us a lot about Roman technology.

Roman roads

The good Roman roads mean that you can travel from one end of the **Empire** to the other. The rulers of Rome need to move soldiers quickly from place to place. Roman roads have smooth surfaces so carts do not get stuck. They are always as straight as possible so travelers take the shortest route.

Having Fun

Everyone gets excited when there are games at the **Colosseum.** This is a huge sports stadium that can hold 50,000 people. In the Colosseum, **gladiators** fight against other gladiators and against wild animals, such as lions and bears. Sand covers the floor to soak up the blood of the gladiators.

At the Circus Maximus you can join many other people to watch exciting and dangerous **chariot** races. You can cheer on the chariot racers as they go around the track at amazing speeds.

The Colosseum is a very special stadium. Its floor can be flooded so that gladiators can fight sea battles.

These are gladiators in training. Some wear armor. Others fight with a spear and must move fast to stay alive.

Going to the theater

There are also more peaceful types of entertainment. Many people go to the theater to watch plays and pantomimes. Roman actors always wear masks. The faces show the type of person the actor is playing. A pantomime is a special type of play where one person tells a story while another acts it out through dance and movements of the face and body.

Roman Rulers

The Roman **Empire** is very large. It is ruled by an **emperor.** Before the rule of the first emperor Augustus, which began in 27 B.C.E., Rome was a **republic.** It was ruled by a group of **citizens** called the **senate.** The senate met at the **forum** in Rome and they help the emperor to run the Empire.

Public officials run each town in the empire. They are elected by Roman citizens. Not everyone is a Roman citizen. Women, children, and slaves cannot be citizens. Citizens can own property and vote in elections. They also have to fight in the Roman army.

Julius Caesar is the most famous Roman general. He conquered Gaul (France) and led an army to Britain in 55 B.C.E.

Trajan's Column in Rome shows scenes of the armies of Emperor Trajan.

The Roman army

The Roman army is the toughest army in the world.
If you meet a soldier, or legionary, he will tell you stories
about the battles he has fought in faraway lands.
The army is divided into **legions** of about 4,000 men.

Roman Religion

The Romans have many different gods. Each one is said to look after a different aspect of people's lives. One goddess, Cardea, is the goddess of doorways and gates! Everybody's house includes a shrine to the household gods, who protect the family and their home.

The Temple of Jupiter in Rome.

Each major god has its own temples and priests. They make sure that the gods are kept happy by organizing sacrifices. The people, even the **emperor,** have to bring animals and food to offer to the gods.

When they add a new place to the **Empire,** the Romans make sure to include its local gods in their worship.

Romans often kept small statues of the gods in their homes. This is a statue of Mars, the god of war.

The Romans believe that the goddess Minerva is the favorite daughter of Jupiter, king of the gods. She is the goddess of skill and wisdom.

Many of the Roman gods are the same as the gods of the ancient Greeks, but with different names.

Celebrations

There are many festivals to celebrate throughout the year. In April, there are bonfires and parties to celebrate the founding of Rome. In August, slaves get a day off in honor of the goddess Diana.

Facts for Romans

Now you know a bit about ancient Rome and its people. Here are a few things you need to know to get by in ancient Rome.

Numbers

The Romans use letters to write numbers. Here are some important numbers:

I – 1   VIII – 8
II – 2   IX – 9
III – 3   X – 10
IV – 4   L - 50
V – 5   C – 100
VI – 6   D – 500
VII – 7   M – 1,000

Measures

Measuring accurately was very important in the great buildings the Romans built:

1 uncia = 0.97 in./2.46cm = one Roman inch

1 pes = about 11.6 in./ 29.5cm = one Roman foot

1 passus = about 1.62 yds/ 1.48m = one Roman pace

1 mille = 1,618 yds/1,480 m = one Roman mile

You will need to know about weights and measures if you go shopping. This is a pharmacist's shop.

Originally, the Roman calendar had ten months. This is why September, October, November, and December mean seven, eight, nine, and ten when for us they are actually the ninth, tenth, eleventh, and twelfth months.

Janus is the god of gateways.

Months of the year

January = Januarius–named after Janus, who has two faces – one looks back to the old year, one looks forward to the new year.

February = Februarius–named after "februare," which means "to purify"

March = Martius–named after Mars, the god of war

April = Aprilis–named after "aperire" which means to "open" and which refers to the opening of flowers

May = Maius–named after Maia, goddess of summer

June = Junius–named after Juno, queen of the gods

July = Julius–named after Julius Caesar (the month of his birth)

August = Augustus–named in honor of emperor Augustus

September = September–the seventh month

October = October–the eighth month

November = November–the ninth month

December = December–the tenth month

Find Out for Yourself

You can not actually travel back in time to ancient Rome but you can still find out a lot about the ancient Romans and how they lived. You will find the answers to some of your questions in this book. You can also use other books and the Internet.

Books to read

Malam, John. *You Wouldn't Want to Be a Roman Gladiator!: Gory Things You'd Rather Not Know*. Danbury, Conn.: Scholastic, 2001.

Steele, Christy. *Rome*. Chicago: Raintree, 2001.

Using the Internet

Explore the Internet to find out more about ancient Rome. Websites can change, so if the link below no longer works, try using a kid-friendly search engine, such as www.yahooligans.com or www.internet4kids.com, and type in keywords such as "villa," "Pompeii," "Roman army," and "Colosseum."

Websites

library.thinkquest.org/CR0210200 Examine ancient cultures on this website. There are fun online activities and sections on various aspects of life in different ancient cultures.

Glossary

aqueduct structure made to move water from one place to another

chariot vehicle with two wheels and pulled by horses

citizen person who lives in a city or town

civilization the way of life of a group of people

Colosseum large stadium for chariot races and gladiator fights

emperor the ruler of an empire

empire land or people living under the command of one ruler

forum center of business

gladiator person who takes part in a fight to the death for public entertainment

landowner owner of land or property such as a field or a house

legion a group of soldiers

mosaic picture made of small pieces of glass or tile

reed tall slender grass found in wet areas

republic type of government where power lies with the citizens through their right to vote

senate group of people that makes laws

temple building for worship

tunic knee-length, belted shirt

wax tablet object used for writing in ancient times

Index

8768

ECHO PARK ELEMENTARY IMC
14100 COUNTY RD 11
BURNSVILLE, MN 55337